HTML

Simplified

The Basics

STEVEN MANN

HTML Simplified – The Basics

Copyright © 2016 by Steven Mann

Trademarks

Warning and Disclaimer

Table of Contents

Introduction

I have noticed through my tutoring efforts that many students, young adults, and adult learners have a need to understand the basics of computing technologies, such as HTML, that is not so daunting. Having worked with these technologies for over twenty years I took it for granted that certain technologies are common knowledge. I was wrong and there is a need for people to learn various computer concepts.

Therefore, I have created this guide book to help people get started with HTML and build a foundation of understanding. This book is geared towards beginners in HTML but does assume general computing skills.

Online Tutoring and Assistance Available

If you need assistance with your HTML, CSS, and/or JavaScript project, you may hire me as a tutor from WyzAnt. My tutor link is below:

http://www.wyzant.com/Tutors/stevetheman

CHAPTER 1

HTML Introduction and Background

Defining HTML

Back in the early 1990's, the World Wide Web (WWW) was born. The Internet was around long before that but having visual web sites which linked content together was a huge step in bringing what the Internet is today.

The abillity for this to happened was based on the creation and interpretation of a web-based language. This language is called **H**yper**T**ext **M**arkup **L**anguage - HTML. Even though the WWW did not gain popularity until the 90's, web pages and HTML were created in the late 1980's.

HTML combines information content with markup tags to present web pages to the user within a web browser. Orginally, most of the content of web pages was text and hyperlinks. The hyperlinks (which have been shortened to be named "links" nowawdays) allowed the user to navigate to other content as they still do today.

Understanding the Tools Needed

HTML Creation

HTML is code within a text-based file. It is human readable and does not need to be compiled into something different. Therefore, any type of text editor will allow you to create HTML pages - even a basic text editor such as Windows NotePad.

There is a more advanced text editor named NotePad++ which may be downloaded for free at https://notepad-plus-plus.org/download/

I recommend using at least NotePad++ as it provides guidance in your markup coding. *The tutorials and screenshots in this guide will be based on the use of NotePad++.*

Many integrated development environment (IDE) software, such as Visual Studio, also supports the creation of HTML files/pages.

HTML Rendering

To run or display your HTML code, you need an internet browser such as Internet Explorer (IE), Google Chrome, or FireFox. NotePad++ allows you run your web page in many different browsers but they need to be installed on your computer.

HTML in the Browser

To tie the creation of HTML code along with the rendering within a browser, a good exercise is as follows:

1. Open up a browser such as Internet Explorer or Google Chrome. (I am using Google Chrome)

2. On your home page (my home page is www.google.com), right click anywhere within the content and select "View page source" as shown below:

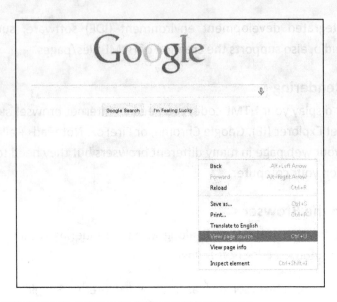

Each browser has a different way of representing the viewing of the source. As a comparison, IE's menu item simply states "View source":

After you select the menu option to view the source, a new window appears with all kinds of code. This is the underyling source of the current web page. The view may be daunting as it may combine HTML and JavaScript together. Don't worry, you will not have to generate this type of code.

3. Close the source window and return to your home page. Press the F12 key on your keyboard. A developer tools window appears and displays the main elements of the web page as shown below in Chrome and IE respectively:

Instead of seeing all of the crazy source code, the Elements view in Chrome or the DOM Explorer in IE only displays the HTML markup code in a contained, organized fashion. These are the core tags and elements that you will be creating within the tutorials of this guide.

CHAPTER 2

Understanding the HTML Document Structure

Understanding Tags

Every HTML element (or object) is defined by using tags. Tags are text within less than and greater than signs ("<>"). Many elements require a begin tag and an end tag. An end tag contains a forward slash ("/") after the less than sign.

The main tag of an HTML file is the HTML tag itself. This provides a container around the other tags such that the browser understands what to render. Therefore a blank HTML page may simply contain the following:

<html>

</html>

The first <html> tag is the begin tag. The </html> is the end tag.

Creating Your First HTML Page

Open up your text editor that you will use in creating your HTML. I will be using NotePad++ as it greatly helps you code HTML files. I highly recommend using it for these tutorials.

If you are using NotePad++, you should tell the program that you will be coding in HTML such that the built-in assistance is provided for you. To do this, click on the Language menu, hover over the H option, and then click on HTML:

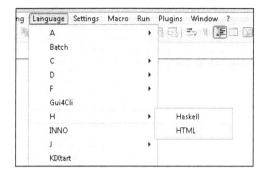

Type in <html> as your first line and then press the Enter key. Press the Enter key several more times to make some space. Next, type </html>.

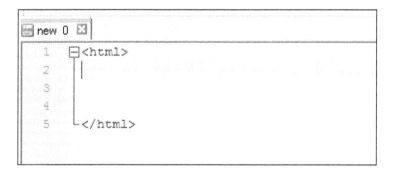

You now have a barebones HTML page. From the File menu, select Save and save your file locally. I recommend creating a new folder under your Documents:

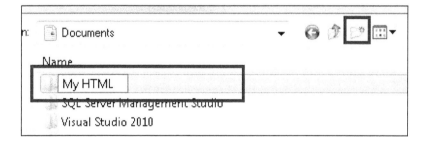

Type in a name for your page such as "My First Page" or "Home Page" and click Save:

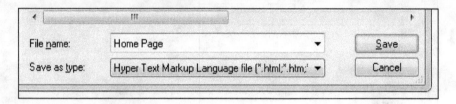

NotePad++ will automatically use .html as the file extension. If you are using a different text editor, you may save it as .html or .htm. Browsers recognize both types of file extensions.

Adding the Core Containers

The HTML tags that you have in your file form the main web page container. Within the main HTML container, there are two sub-containers that should be created. These are the body and head.

You can visualize these as boxes where HTML is the main box that contains two "smaller" boxes of head and body:

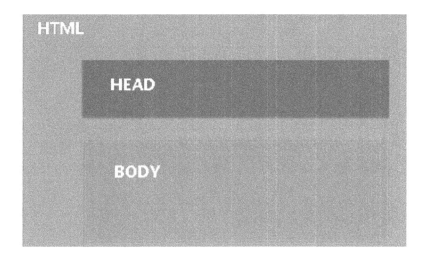

The head section is used to provide the browser with page instructions such as style libraries (CSS) and JavaScript file (.js) references. The body section is where the main content lives and where most of the tags and markup you learn in this guide will be placed.

Within your new web page, add the head and body tags as shown:

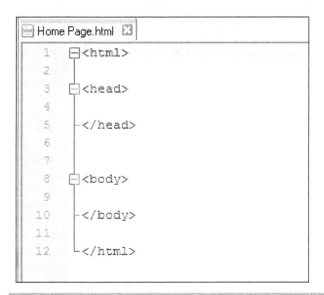

Adding Initial Content and Markup

Head

In the head section, you may use a title tag to name the web page. This determines what the browser displays within the web page browser tab. Within the head section of your web page, enter a title line as follows:

<title>My First Web Page</title>

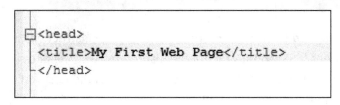

```
<head>
  <title>My First Web Page</title>
</head>
```

Body

The body contains the content that is displayed on the web page itself. You could simply just type text in here and it will display. However there is a <p> tag that is used to determine paragraphs within your textual content. Within the body section of your web page enter the following:

<p>My First Web Page Content</p>

```
<body>
  <p>My First Web Page Content</p>
</body>
```

Web Page Check

At this point, your web page markup should look something similar to the following:

```
1    <html>
2    <head>
3      <title>My First Web Page</title>
4    </head>
5    <body>
6      <p>My First Web Page Content</p>
7    </body>
8    </html>
```

Save your changes.

Rendering Your First Web Page

If you are using NotePad++ you may run your web page by simply se-
lecting to launch in your browser of choice from the Run menu:

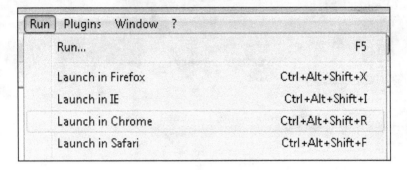

If you are not using NotePad++, navigate to your web page file on your
computer (the place where you saved the file):

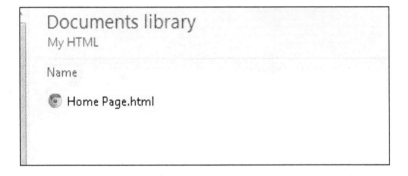

If the icon looks like Chrome such as in my case or a web page, you may
simply double-click the file to launch your web page within a browser.
Otherwise you may right-click the file, select Open With, and then select
an available browser.

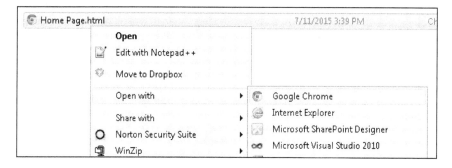

Once you launch your web page, the browser will open your HTML as a file:

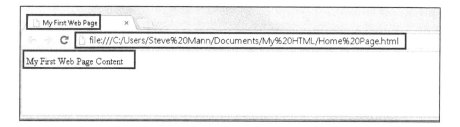

The tab title contains the text that you used within the <title> tags and the content displays the text you used within the <p> tags.

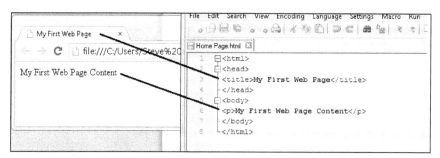

Great! You have your first basic web page created!

CHAPTER 3

Formatting Textual Content

Using Headlines

The text content that rendered in your page is pretty small and just, well, plain. In HTML there are predefined headline instructions to make larger bold text appear.

There are actually six (6) different variations of headlines numbered from 1 through 6. As the number increases, the size of the text decreases.

The tags for these headlines are as follows:

<h1>

<h2>

<h3>

<h4>

<h5>

<h6>

Most web pages and content typical only use the first three headline types but all six are available if needed.

In your web page, change the <p> tags to <h1> tags as follows:

<h1>My First Web Page Content</h1>

```
<body>
  <h1>My First Web Page Content</h1>
</body>
```

Save your web page and launch it within a browser:

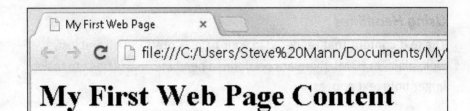

See the difference? Great!

You can play with the various sizes from 1 through 6:

```
<body>
<h1>My First Web Page Content</h1>
<h2>My First Web Page Content</h2>
<h3>My First Web Page Content</h3>
<h4>My First Web Page Content</h4>
<h5>My First Web Page Content</h5>
<h6>My First Web Page Content</h6>
</body>
```

My First Web Page Content

My First Web Page Content

My First Web Page Content

My First Web Page Content

My First Web Page Content

My First Web Page Content

Using Text Decoration Tags

The headline tags are great for segmenting content but you may also want to format the plain text within that content. You may easily perform standard formatting (bold, italic, underline) using the available text decoration tags, also referred to as phrase tags.

Bold

By using the <b> tag, you can make text bold within your content:

<b>This is bold text using the b tag</b>

```
<h1>My First Web Page Content</h1>
<p>
<b>This is bold text using the b tag</b>
</p>
```

My First Web Page Content

This is bold text using the b tag

As in other areas of coding and technology, there are sometimes two ways of accomplishing the same thing. You may also use the <strong> tag to make text bold:

<strong>This is bold text using the strong tag</strong>

```
<body>
 <h1>My First Web Page Content</h1>
<p>
 <b>This is bold text using the b tag</b>
 <strong>This is bold text using the strong tag</strong>
 </p>
 </body>
```

My First Web Page Content

This is bold text using the b tag This is bold text using the strong tag

As you can see, both the <b> and the <strong> produce the same results. Hmmm, I placed both of those examples on separate lines but it rendered all together...

Line Breaks

When working with textual content (as well as other HTML elements), the browser reads and renders the text as one long line. In many cases, just because you hit Enter and place HTML on a new line doesn't mean the browser will render this on a new line.

This is because the browser essential reads your web page HTML as one long string ignoring spaces and line breaks. Therefore, there are times when you need to force a line break.

To force a line break, use the <br/> tag. This is considered an "empty" tag as there are no begin and end tags. The tag is self-contained and does not act as a container of other content such as <body>, <h1>, or <p>.

Place a <br/> tag in your HTML to see the affects:

```
<h1>My First Web Page Content</h1>
<p>
<b>This is bold text using the b tag</b><br/>
<strong>This is bold text using the strong tag</strong>
</p>
</body>
```

My First Web Page Content

This is bold text using the b tag
This is bold text using the strong tag

Now each sentence appears on a separate line.

Italic
You may make text italic by using the <i> tag for italic or <em> for emphasized text. They both produce the same result similar to <b> and <strong>:

`<i>This is italic text using the i tag</i><br/>`

`<em>This is italic text using the em tag</em>`

My markup now looks like this (notice I added some more `<br/>` tags to produce line breaks):

```
<p>
  <b>This is bold text using the b tag.</b><br/>
  <strong>This is also bold text using the strong tag</strong><br/>
  <i>This is italic text using the i tag.</i><br/>
  <em>This is also italic text using the em tag</em><br/>
</p>
```

My First Web Page Content

This is bold text using the b tag
This is bold text using the strong tag
This is italic text using the i tag
This is italic text using the em tag

Underline

It is possible to also underline your text by using the <u> tag:

<u>Only u can make me underline</u>

```
<p>
<b>This is bold text using the b tag.</b><br/>
<strong>This is also bold text using the strong tag</strong><br/>
<i>This is italic text using the i tag.</i><br/>
<em>This is also italic text using the em tag</em><br/>
<u>Only u can make me underline</u>
</p>
```

My First Web Page Content

This is bold text using the b tag
This is bold text using the strong tag
This is italic text using the i tag
This is italic text using the em tag
<u>*Only u can make me underline*</u>

Paragraphs

Originally you used the <p> tag to present the original text content. I just wanted to recap the paragraph tag again and show how it may be used instead of line breaks.

I therefore removed the line break tags and segmented my content into three different paragraphs:

<p>

<b>This is bold text using the b tag.</b><strong>This is also bold text using the strong tag</strong>

</p>

<p>

<i>This is italic text using the i tag.</i><em>This is also italic text using the em tag</em>

</p>

<p>

<u>Only u can make me underline</u>

</p>

```
<p>
<b>This is bold text using the b tag.</b>
<strong>This is also bold text using the strong tag</strong>
</p>
<p>
<i>This is italic text using the i tag.</i>
<em>This is also italic text using the em tag</em>
</p>
<p>
<u>Only u can make me underline</u>
</p>
```

The browser places a line break after each paragraph:

My First Web Page Content

This is bold text using the b tag. This is also bold text using the strong tag

This is italic text using the i tag. This is also italic text using the em tag

<u>Only u can make me underline</u>

Other Text Decorations

Other text decorations may be achieved using inline styles or CSS. The inline styles are explained in Chapter . The CSS styles are explained in my ***CSS Simplified*** book.

Producing Content in Lists

To make content easily consumable by the reader, you may want pre-sent content in lists. Using HTML tags you may accomplish list formatting using either a bulleted list or numbered/lettered list.

A bulleted list is called an unordered list and a numbered/lettered list is called an ordered list.

Both of this list types are achieved by various HTML tags. The first tag represents the list container and the second tag is used to identify each item in the list.

Bulleted List (Unordered List)

To create a bulleted list, you place list items into an unordered list container. The unordered list container is as follows:

<ul>

</ul>

The list items are designated within <li> tags as follows:

<ul>

<li>List Item 1</li>

<li>List Item 2</li>

<li> List Item 3</li>

</ul>

In your web page markup, add a few line breaks and then create a bulleted list:

```
</p>
<br/><br/>
<p>Here is my bulleted list of important items:</p>
<ul>
<li>List Item 1</li>
<li>List Item 2</li>
<li> List Item 3</li>
</ul>
```

Here is my bulleted list of important items:

- List Item 1
- List Item 2
- List Item 3

Numbered/Lettered List (Ordered List)

To create a numbered or lettered list, you place list items into an ordered list container. The ordered list container is as follows:

<ol>

</ol>

The list items are designated within <li> tags as follows:

<ol>

<li>List Item 1</li>

<li>List Item 2</li>

<li> List Item 3</li>

</ol>

In your web page markup, add a few line breaks and then create an ordered list:

```
<br/><br/>
<p>Here is my numbered list of important items:</p>
<ol>
<li>List Item 1</li>
<li>List Item 2</li>
<li> List Item 3</li>
</ol>
```

> Here is my numbered list of important items:
>
> 1. List Item 1
> 2. List Item 2
> 3. List Item 3

<ol> produces a numbered list by default.

To produce a lettered list of items, add type="A" to the <ol> tag:

<ol type="A">

<li>List Item 1</li>

<li>List Item 2</li>

<li> List Item 3</li>

</ol>

```
<br/><br/>
<p>Here is my lettered list of important items:</p>
<ol type="A">
<li>List Item 1</li>
<li>List Item 2</li>
<li> List Item 3</li>
</ol>
```

Here is my lettered list of important items:

    A. List Item 1
    B. List Item 2
    C. List Item 3

CHAPTER 4

Displaying a Picture

Creating an Image Page

To keep things separated as well as to have more than one page for creating links in the next chapter, create a new HTML web page using your text editor and call it My Image Page:

<html>

<head>

<title>My Image Page</title>

</head>

<body>

<h1>My Image Page</h1>

</body>

</html>

```
Home Page.html ☒  My Image Page.html ☒
 1   <html>
 2   <head>
 3    <title>My Image Page</title>
 4   </head>
 5
 6   <body>
 7    <h1>My Image Page</h1>
 8
 9   </body>
10
11
12   </html>
```

Adding a Picture to Your Page

Physical File

Find a picture you would like to use and copy the physical file to your HTML folder where you are creating your web pages:

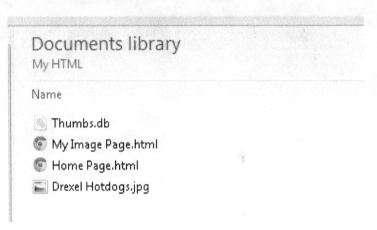

I am going to use my Drexel Hotdogs photo for this example.

Picture Markup

Pictures are added to web pages by using the image tag <img>. The image tag is one of those empty tags that do not provide a container for anything else.

To add a picture to your page, the simplest markup is as follows:

<img src='Drexel Hotdogs.jpg' />

```
<body>
  <h1>My Image Page</h1>
  <img src='Drexel Hotdogs.jpg' />
</body>
```

My Image Page

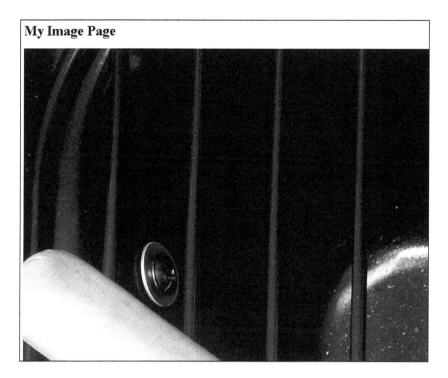

It looks like my photo is very large. This is the case in using high-res photos on your web pages. Therefore it is a good idea to include the width and height attributes. Sometimes you may just want have the width attribute to keep the image in proportion.

Add a width and height attribute to the <img> tag:

<img src='Drexel Hotdogs.jpg' width="400px" height="200px" />

```
<body>
  <h1>My Image Page</h1>
  <img src='Drexel Hotdogs.jpg' width="400px" height="200px" />
  <br/>
  <img src='Drexel Hotdogs.jpg' width="400px" />
```

I am going to experiment and include an image with just the width to see the difference.

My Image Page

SRC Attribute

By just entering the name of the photo in the source (src), the browser assumes the location of the picture file is the same as the web page location. Many times this is not the case and therefore the path to the picture file is also included.

To demonstrate this in a simple fashion, create a new folder within your HTML folder named "images" and move your photo into that folder:

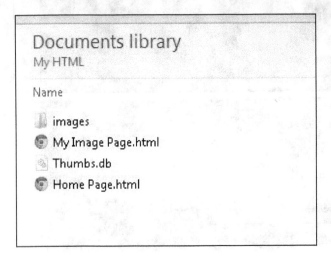

Now your photo lives under ./images relative to the web page.

If you attempt to render your image web page now, you will see a broken image:

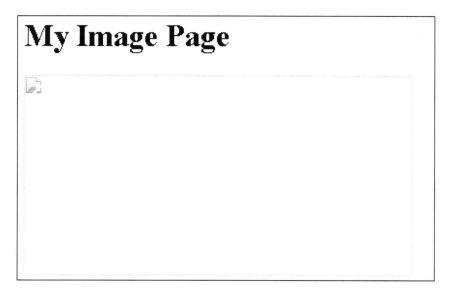

If you include an alt attribute in your image tag, this is a case where it will display:

<img src='Drexel Hotdogs.jpg' width="400px" height="200px" alt="Hotdogs" />

```
<body>
  <h1>My Image Page</h1>
  <img src='Drexel Hotdogs.jpg' width="400px" height="200px" alt="Hotdogs" />
  <br/>
```

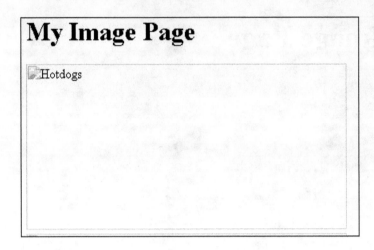

To fix the broken image, add the images folder location within the src attribute of the image tag:

<img src='images/Drexel Hotdogs.jpg' width="400px" height="200px" alt="Hotdogs" />

```
<body>
  <h1>My Image Page</h1>
  <img src='images/Drexel Hotdogs.jpg'
</body>
```

My Image Page

ALL GOOD!!!

CHAPTER 5

Understanding Block versus Inline Elements

Introduction

Understanding block versus inline elements helps a great deal when attempting to align and position your content within your web page. I never really cared until I needed to produce more complicated content arrangements.

Block Elements

Block elements, also referred to as block level elements, take up the entire width of their parent container. By default the main parent container is the <body> of the html page which takes up the entire browser window.

Inline Elements

Inline elements only takes up the space that they exist based on their contents.

The span tag, <span>, is an inline element. It is generic meaning it does not have any default styles. When you need to keep text together inline, the span tag assists.

Paragraph tag <p> as explained in Chapter 3, is a block element. When you have paragraphs of text to display, use this tag to contain that text and spread over the width of the parent container.

Demonstration

To illustrate the difference, I went onto codepen.io to create an example. You may see the example yourself here:
http://codepen.io/stevethemanmann/pen/grPvPw

You may also see a listing of my Code Pens on my blog:
www.stevethemanmann.com

In my HTML, I have two <div>'s. <div>'s are block elements so without styling, they take up the entire width of the <body>. In the first <div>, I have two <p> elements. Since <p> elements are also block elements, even though I only have a handful of text, they take up the entire width of their parent divs.

```
<div>
   <p>This is the p tag</p>
   <p>And other p tag</p>
</div>
```

Therefore, the results are two lines of words:

This is the p tag

And other p tag

In my second <div>, I used two <span>'s in place of the <p>'s:

```
<div>
    <span>This is the span tag</span>
    <span>And other span tag</span>
</div>
```

But now since the <span>'s are inline, they do not take up the entire width of the parent <div>. Thus, the two lines of words are rendered next to each other:

This is the span tag And other span tag

The complete example is shown below:

```
HTML                                        Tidy  ✖
<div>
    <p>This is the p tag</p>
    <p>And other p tag</p>
</div>
<br>
<div>
    <span>This is the span tag</span>
    <span>And other span tag</span>
</div>
```

This is the p tag

And other p tag

This is the span tag And other span tag

Conclusion

This book explored the very beginner basics of coding in HTML. In addition, several foundational concepts were explained. Readers should now understand HTML concepts and basic coding principles such that they may build upon their skills with more advanced coding.

ABOUT THE AUTHOR

Steve Mann was born and raised in Philadelphia, Pennsylvania, where he still resides. He is an Enterprise Application Engineer for Morgan Lewis and has more than 20 years of professional experience. He has authored and co-authored several books related to collaboration technology. Steve graduated Drexel University in 1993 and 2015 majoring in Information Systems.

Steve's blog site can be found at: www.SteveTheManMann.com

Follow Steve on Twitter @stevethemanmann

Online Tutoring and Assistance Available

If you need assistance with your HTML, CSS, and/or JavaScript project, you may hire Steve as a tutor from WyzAnt. His tutor link is below:

http://www.wyzant.com/Tutors/stevetheman